AF252125

A Tarantella On a Cloud

by

PANSYE H. POWELL

THE GOLDEN QUILL PRESS
Publishers
Francestown   New Hampshire

Library of Congress Catalog Card Number 76-1223

ISBN 0-8233-0239-3

Printed in the United States of America

For MIKE

ACKNOWLEDGMENTS

The poems in this collection have, with few exceptions, been published. For permission to reprint, the author is grateful to the following: *Child Life; Children's Friend; Denver Post; Deseret News; Ideals; Mayflower Log; Philadelphia Bulletin; Portland Oregonian;* Radio Program, "A Tribute to the Poets;" *Relief Society Magazine; Salt Lake Tribune;* Award Booklet of Utah State Institute of Fine Arts; *Wall Street Journal;* and *Writer's Digest.*

CONTENTS

REFLECTIONS ON THE HUMAN CONDITION

FOR THE GERIATRIC SET

A TARANTELLA ON A CLOUD

"You're growing old," my body said to me;
"The crow's-feet gather, and the moments crowd."
"So what of that?" my spirit crowed in glee,
And danced a tarantella on a cloud!

NOTE TO ANYONE OVER FIFTY

Take a timely tip
From an omnipresent weed —
The dandelion's hair turns white
Because it goes to seed!

TEMPUS FUGIT

No longer can folks like you and me
Conceal the number of our days
Since we have lived enough to see
Another ukelele craze.

THE UNTAMED POOCH

"I'm going to walk the dog," I said
And set out jauntingly;
But Sneakers had other ideas —
He soon was walking me!

DE SENECTUTE

Aging is human; loving's divine.
How fortunate when they combine!

ENUF'S ENUF

We've been on a nostalgic binge,
Amounting to an obsession,
But isn't it going a bit too far
To bring back the depression?

HELP! HELP!

Bottle caps are made secure
For protection of small fry
Who might become inquisitive,
And surely that is why
Folks in second childhood
Simply cannot pry
Those lids off, no matter how
Desperately they try!

SURE SIGN

She may say she is ailing,
She may sigh and complain,
She may talk about twinges
And rail at the rain.
Though she grumbles and grunts,
You may bet money on it;
There's life in her yet —
See that brand-new spring bonnet?

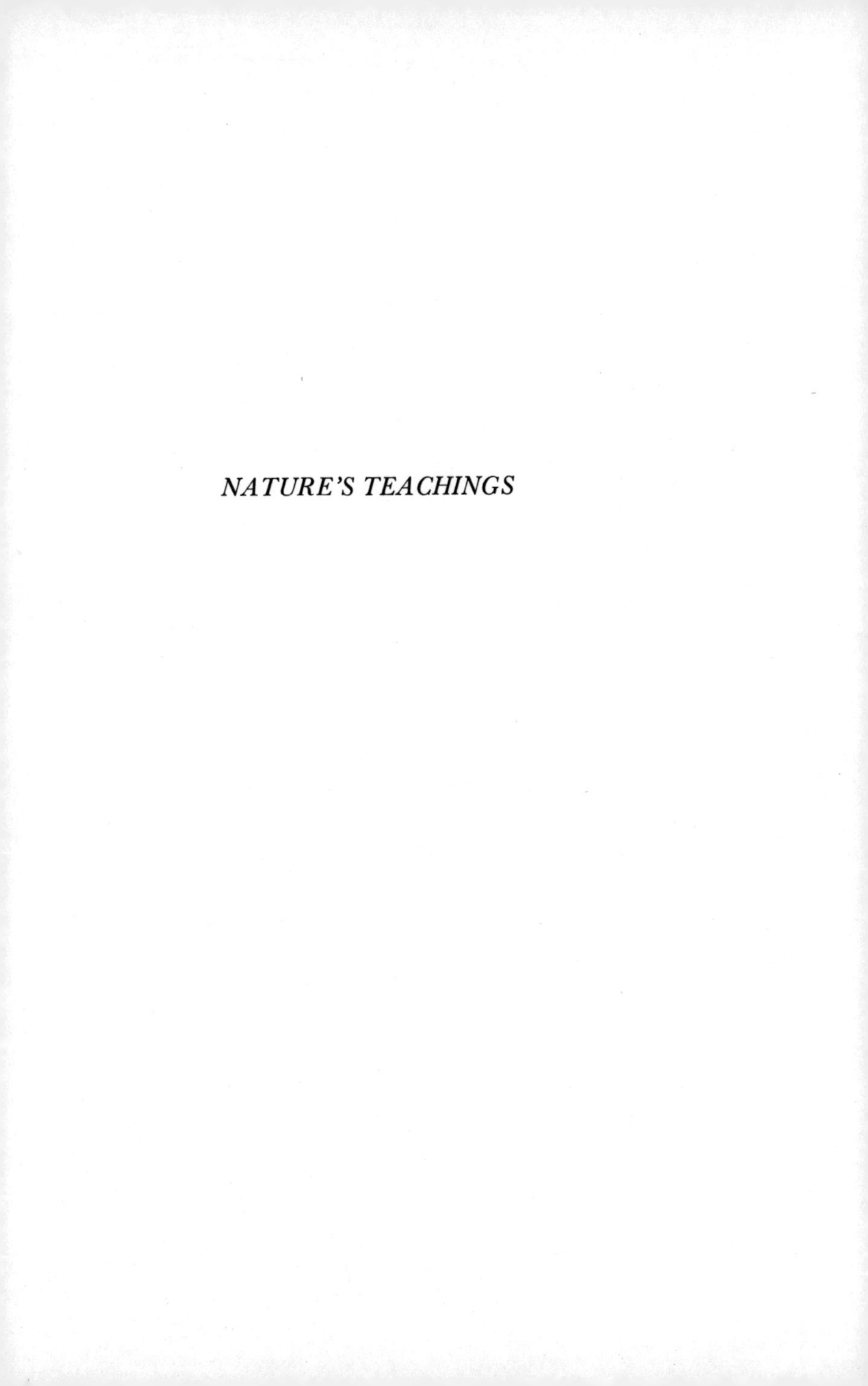

NATURE'S TEACHINGS

GEODE

I passed it by, but he was wise —
My friend, the geologist.
He opened the rock my careless eyes
Had noticed only to despise,
And found amethyst!

POOL

Blue
As the morning glory,
The sloping walls of the pool
Fashion a flower-shaped cup to catch
Day dreams.

EARLY RISERS

Dame Nature's been asleep,
Her snow cap on her head.
She'd like to snooze a little more,
But now must tend instead
Those naughty little hyacinths
That will not stay in bed!

PRECAUTION

When hourly the wild goose trumpet calls
And sheep press close in fold,
The mountains put on their paisley shawls
To keep them safe from cold!

U. N.

When my flower beds are blooming,
My iris and its relations
Will present in many-colored flags
Their own United Nations!

ROYAL RAIMENT

Regal the garments my city will wear
When nature has dressed her in robes as of old;
Kingly the colors my city will bear:
Lilacs for purple and jonquils for gold.

COPY-CATS

When little girls go out to play,
They like to copy grown-ups' way.
Piling high their curly tresses,
Donning heels and trailing dresses,
They try with studied mincing pace
To simulate their sisters' grace.

So the littlest maple trees-es
Flaunt yellow scarves in autumn breezes,
And like their oldsters, fashion-wise,
Touch golden tips with scarlet dyes,
Until each stands in mimic state —
A miniature tree fashion-plate.

SPRING SHOW

Nature's preparing a special treat,
Free for the eyes of all to meet,
Someday soon in the early spring —
The tulips' annual opening.

ON GUARD

When summer nights hold clover-sweets,
Beset by insect vandals,
Then firefly watchmen light their beats
With flashing neon candles!

A HINT

Nature's proportions are always just,
So man is not nature's freak —
Two eyes to see, two ears to hear,
But only one mouth to speak!

ON THE BUSINESS OF WORD-USAGE

EGGZACTLY

Grammarians argue the pros and the cons,
But a farmer can tell them what's fitting,
For anyone knows a hen can sit without setting,
But never can set without sitting.

ECONOMY

I thought that I should write a sonnet,
But reason promptly frowned upon it —
When I can put my thought in four,
Why stretch it out for ten lines more?

A WORD TO THE WISE

Sappho sighed her love in song,
While Penelope
Wove a web the whole day long,
Fraught with memory.

Sappho's words will e'er accuse her,
But no shadows lurk
Around fair Penny to abuse her —
She tore up her work!

OUR NATIVES' TONGUE

English, as it is spoken
In some parts, it is true,
Gives rise to many questions
And calculations, too:

> How far is *all the farther*?
> How many are *quite a few*?
> And if one's *in a dither*
> Is he cooler than *in a stew*?

PITY THE POOR FOREIGNER

Pity the man who tries to learn
The idioms that abound
In English speech, for strange indeed
The paradoxes found —
A man lies while he stands,
A hen sits when she sets,
And we raze an old house to the ground!

PENNY PINCHING

I wrote
A poem
That looked
Like this.
I thought
For sure
It could
Not miss,
For line
By line,
I thought
To learn
The cash
My poem
Would sure-
Ly earn.
But when
It saw
The print
Of day,
The lines were doubled up this way!

ON FORBIDDEN TOPICS

One editor's all for women's lib;
A second despises Adam's rib.
A third likes a frisky porno bit,
But a fourth will not have a word of "it."
Politics must be taboo,
Religion and ethnic bias, too.
So many topics he must eschew —
What is the hungry bard to do
But in self-defense bow down to fate
Or remain in his unpublished state?

HINTS TO A MODERN READER

What used to be a magalopolis
Is now a conurbation.
A good old-fashioned argument
Is today a confrontation.
Gentle Reader must learn to cope
With new terms like anomic,
With neutron and isotrope
In an era gone atomic.
If he comes upon entrophication,
Dear Reader may think that he
Is under an hallucination
That words such as this can be.
If he's to read what has been written,
With reference-itis he must be smitten.

CONCERNING SMALL FRY

WHEN THE CIRCUS COMES TO TOWN

I like to go on picnics
    And to outdoor movies, too;
It's fun to splash in swimming pools
    And visit at the zoo.
But the best time's every summer
    When my daddy takes me down
To watch the folks parading
    When the circus comes to town!

Oh, the ladies on the horses
    Are all rosy cheeks and smiles,
And the colored wagons seem to pass
    For miles and miles and miles.
The elephants are big and gray;
    Their riders all are brown —
Oh, there's nothing like the people
    When the circus comes to town!

There are Indians and cowboys
    With their guns and lariats.
There are cunning Shetland ponies,
    And the horses all wear hats!
There are dancing dogs and monkeys
    And a silly floppy clown —
Oh, there's nothing quite so funny
    As when the circus comes to town.

The peanuts and the popcorn
    And the sugar-candy foam

Taste better than the things I eat
    When I am back at home.
My daddy buys them for me
    And my mommy doesn't frown —
Oh, the best time of the whole year's
    When the circus comes to town!

YOUNG EXPERT

My grandson's an authority
On hockey teams of all degree.
Each game he watches on t. v.
Is the battle of the century.
Various players he can spot 'n
Once they're seen, they're not forgotten.
The garage is cluttered with sticks and masks
And gloves and pucks, and still he asks
For new equipment. He buys the lore,
Cons it well, and yells for more.
The collection of bruises and swollen joints
His mother frequently anoints
Are trophies of the sidewalk frays
With which he occupies his days.
Would as studiously he'd stick
To readin', writin', and 'rithmetic!

HERO

My brother wears a uniform;
He shines the buttons every day,
And every night when he comes home
He puts it carefully away.

My brother's uniform is brown
Because he's in the Army now;
I'd like to shoot his big old gun —
Someday, he says, he'll show me how.

I think my brother's an officer,
Or else he's going to be.
I know the letters on his coat —
They spell R. O. T. C.

MOTHER'S HELPER

He travels in a realm few adults know,
A far-off land where seneschals and churls
Are laborers. There every noble whirls
Away on a prancing steed, and gay knights go
To keep their trysts with lady-love or foe
Across a drawbridge. A servile hind unfurls
His master's pennon, scarlet-bright, that swirls
In sweeping folds above his helmet's glow.

How could I dare to go where fancy soars,
Where ballad-singing minstrels greet the dawn,
Where tourneys are the proving of a man?
How could I ask Sir Launcelot or Bors
To carry groceries or mow the lawn
Or burn the trash that floods my garbage can?

NO DUPLICATIONS

Last year we saw a Santa Claus
On every other street.
They promised Junior such rewards
We found them hard to meet.

This year I advocate a sign
To pin upon small fry:
"This child has seen one Santa Claus —
Please let him pass on by."

CALLERS

The doorbell rang at half-past three.
They came, they said, to visit me.
They sat upon the long divan,
Preserving silence to a man.
Their eyes were glued upon one spot,
For one whole hour observed me not.
They took no tea. At half-past four
They rose and walked out my front door.
Tomorrow, they'll repeat these tricks —
Three boys, aged eight and five and six,
Will view in a hypnotic row
The television cartoon show!

EARTH-WALK

When we travel with Meghan, aged three, we deplore
That she has a strong proclivity
For restrooms — and consequently more
Extra-vehicular activity!

THE LONG AND SHORT OF IT

We cut our Meghan's hair today —
It was her pride and joy —
But how could we let our little girl
Go looking like a boy?

ADVICE TO A COWBOY

Your leather pants fit perfectly;
Your hat is broad, as it should be.
Your red checked shirt's authentic, too —
In spite of all, I know it's you,
So get that gun out of my ribs —
Real cowboys never wear pink bibs!

ARTIST IN THE KITCHEN

Jack is given honors
For the pictures he can make,
But the artist is my mother
Who knows how to frost a cake!

TO A LITTLE GIRL ON SUNDAY

Little girl so clean and sweet,
In pinafore all starched and neat,
With Mary Janes upon your feet,
Oh, what a shame to see you treat
Your clothes to sliding on concrete
And playing leapfrog in the street!

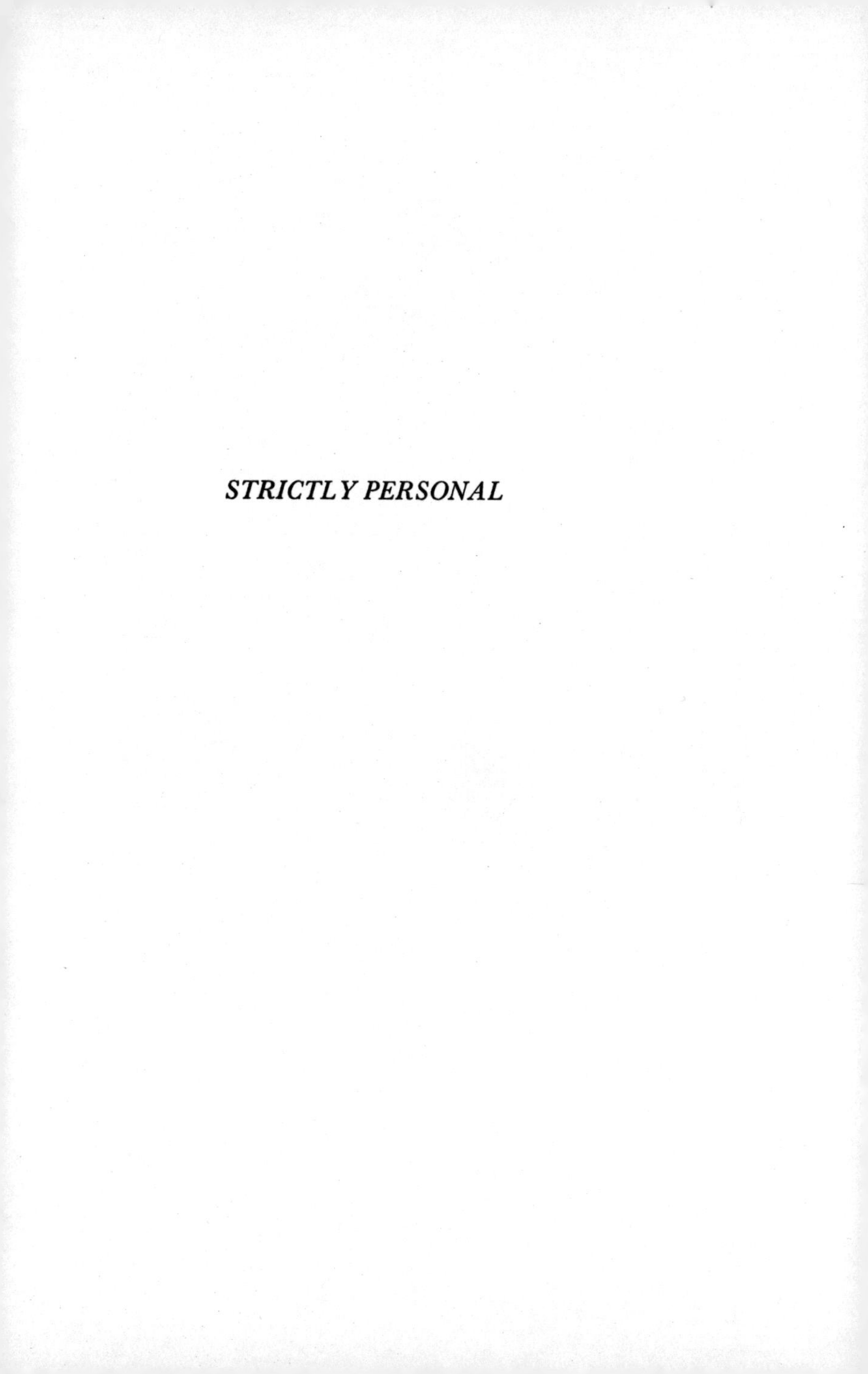

STRICTLY PERSONAL

QUESTION

Shall I walk up a golden stair
And have a jeweled crown to wear?
And be on blessed manna fed?
And have cloud-pillows on my bed?
Shall I play on a harp of gold
And still be young when I am old?
And wear a robe of purest white
When I hang out the stars at night?
Well — if it's going to be like this,
It's not my dream of heavenly bliss!

INDIAN GIVER

I'm very much ashamed of me,
I tell it with a moan —
I bought a gift to give away
And kept it for my own.

SCHOOLMA'AM'S COMMENT

Sometimes I lead triumphant hordes
To fame where all may see us,
And sometimes drive reluctant herds
In the manner of Eumaeus.

STREET ENCOUNTER

When some seedy-looking bloke
Asks me, "Can you spare a dime?"
I say to him, "You know who's broke?
......................................I'm!"

MOVING DAY

There are books in all the canisters,
And bras where there ought to be slippers.
Sheets are draped over the banisters;
The egg beater's in a box of zippers.

I think my checkbook's in the foot locker —
Along with the cracker tray.
Now, don't conclude I'm off my rocker —
This is my normal moving day!

PLANE TALK
(Written B.D.D. — Before Detection Devices)

I've always trusted my fellow man,
But on airplanes no longer feel I can.
I view all riders with gimlet eye,
And draw conclusions as they pass by.
That briefcase in hand very well might be
Hiding a bomb to bring misery.
Women's purses every one
Could easily conceal a gun.
Why I watch them is plain to see —
I wonder why they're watching me!

A MAIDEN'S DILEMMA

He is handsome and suave and he's cultured and neat.
He is clever and dapper and gentle and sweet.
He is lithe as a panther, and light on his feet —
But he just won't do for me.

He owns a car, a farm, and a house.
He is too much a man to be ever a mouse.
He is just what a girl should want in a spouse —
But he just won't do for me.

He is skilled in his business, expert in a trade,
And he knows all the ways of a man with a maid.
He'll be faithful in love though his sweetheart may fade —
But he just won't do for me.

Oh, dear, I'm afraid that a spinster I'll be,
For I never shall find one congenial as he,
But he was born under Leo and I, Aries,
So he just won't do for me.

POET'S PLEA

Some folks "dig" the latest jive,
Others learn the jack-knife dive.
Females of the species bake,
Swim a channel, tame a snake,
While their masters grow a beard,
Or do other things as weird.
Since each has a pet delight
He pursues from morn to night,
Pray allow me this confession
Of my form of self-expression.

PROGRESS

Great-grandmother lived in a cabin home,
And Grandma, a cottage small;
Mother's house was an elegant place —
Mine's just a hole in the wall.

Great-grandmother cooked on a brick fireplace,
And Grandma, a kitchen range;
Mother's stove was electrical —
If I ever cook, it's strange!

Great-grandmother's hoe cake won her fame,
And Grandma's biscuits brown;
Mother baked many a crispy loaf —
I buy my bread in town.

Great-grandmother helped her husband plow,
And Grandma hoed garden hills;
Mother watered posy beds —
I tend two pots on the sills!

ON COMPLETING A RECENT NOVEL

Won't someone serve me toast and tea
And bring me back to normalcy?
Please exorcise my schizophrenia
Before I yield to neurasthenia.
Frankly, I have serious doubt
That I shall live the evening out,
For I have dwelt vicariously
With all perversities that be.
Wherefore, strike up the common note —
I need a potent antidote.

NOTES ON REARING A CHILD

I

When you were born, I thought you'd be
A great man for a certainty,
Ambassador-at-large, or such —
I thought I'd not expect too much.
But now you're twenty-one, all hail!
You've managed to stay out of jail.

II

The Swedish have an adage
That keeps reminding me:
"The apple never falls
Far distant from the tree!"

ANNUAL REFLECTION

The grocer's bill is over due;
The rent has gone a-begging;
I owe the milkman's charges, too —
I'm sure that tongues are wagging.

Perennially this is my fate,
On current bills I'm lax;
But Uncle Sam won't have to wait —
I pay my income tax.

FIRST DATE

Johnny is having his first date tonight,
    So I, like a sensible mother,
Have scrubbed his ears and dolled him up right
    To watch him step out with another.

The thoughts in my mind would stagger belief,
    I should tell them with great hesitating.
Oh, tell me, I pray, is there never relief
    For a parent whose offspring is dating?

ALAS

Shakespeare I study and Chaucer,
And Milton and Byron and Keats.
I bow in humble obeisance
Before their poetical feats.

Teasdale and Millay and Jeffers
And Sandburg I read with all ease,
But when I compose, all I utter
Is doggerel verses like these!

CONFESSION

Of things that I wouldn't do or be
I've a list that would stagger a Pharisee.
I wouldn't hold hands while walking the street,
Though that is the action of many I meet.
I wouldn't want to be a squatter
Because I shouldn't think I oughter
(But I'd stay in once I got in,
If I had a place to squat in.)
Though I admire a good technician,
I'd never envy a mortician;
Though his is such a needful chore,
There are things I'd rather do much more.
I'd never want to be a preacher,
A deacon, or a Sunday teacher.
In fact, prosaic though I be
I'm mighty satisfied with ME.

NEW LINES TO AN OLD TUNE

Oh, my darling, oh, my darling,
Oh, my darling midriff line!
Thou art lost and gone forever,
Woe is me, oh, woe is mine!

UNRESTRAINED COMMENT

It's not the price of girdles
        Makes me weep —
It's not initial cost,
        It's UPCREEP!

ANATHEMA

People I like less
Than these are very few:
Those who consider me guilty
Of things they themselves would do!

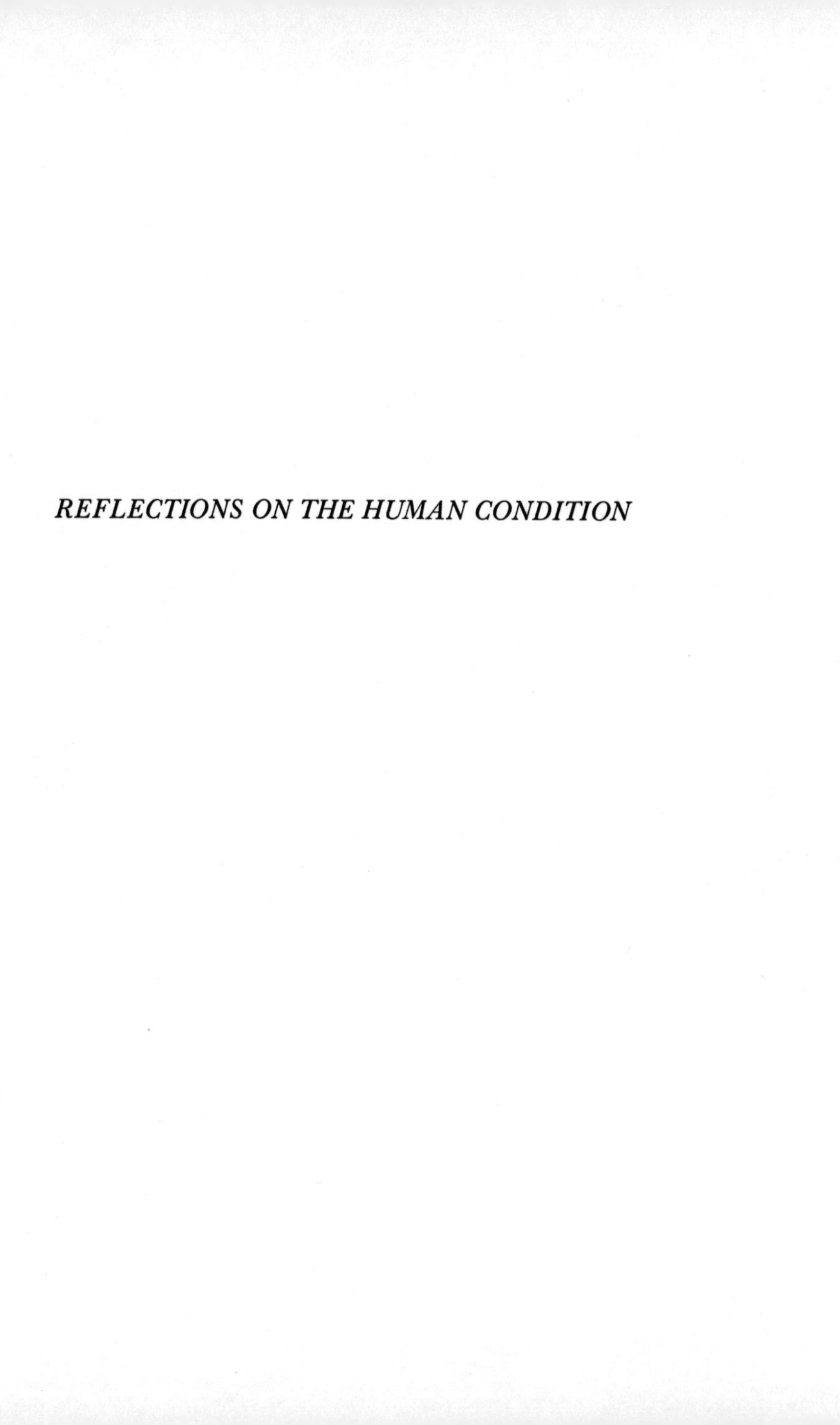

REFLECTIONS ON THE HUMAN CONDITION

ALWAYS THE ROSES

Perennially the roses bloom
    And June brides walk the aisle.
As certainly high taxes loom,
    And modistes change the style.

Nothing in life was even new
    When Sappho tuned her lyre,
And the smoke went up the chimney flue
    In Babylon and Tyre.

Life was ever thus, we know —
    Accept it as we should,
Nor try to change the *status quo*
    . . . As if we could!

EPITAPH

Here lies the body of Jonathan Sweet,
Who stood on the curbing and not in the street.
He crossed on the green instead of the red,
He never was known to smoke in his bed.
He never touched light wires while taking a bath;
Greater discretion no man ever hath.
Now you may believe he died in his bed
Of natural causes. The fact is — he did!

YOU CAN TAKE IT WITH YOU

China dogs and green-clad elves
Sitting on my parlor shelves;
Dresden figurines and such
Cluttering my maple hutch;
Brass from New York's ghetto side,
Opium pipe and zebra hide —
All collecting lint each day,
Steal my precious hours away.
Serapes must be shaken clean,
Japanese prints and Indian screen
Cry for dusting while I sigh
For leisure moments now gone by.

Why, oh, why did no one say,
"These are not for sale today"?
Then I wouldn't be a slave,
Driven to a what-not grave!

THE LIBERATED

She wants to be a fireman,
A deep-sea diver, too.
She knows that she'd be excellent
As keeper in a zoo.

She wants to take on every job
Once handled by her master —
To some, her omnipresence bodes
National disaster.

But there is one important task
With which she doesn't bother —
She knows she is not qualified.
She cannot be a father!

UNION FOREVER

Scorn not the brief conjunction *and*.
It is a potent, able band,
Combining words of all degree
In amicable unity:

> Ham and eggs
> Sugar and spice
> Bread and butter
> Soda and ice
> Cash and carry
> Black and white
> Grin and bear it
> Day and night
> Salt and pepper
> Buttons and bows
> Skull and crossbones
> Fingers and toes

And so it goes *ad infinitum*
The list is long if you wish to write 'em,
But the best use of *and* that I can see
Is to tie together you AND me!

THE MISSING LINK

In spite of virtuous living
And a spirit most forgiving,
I meet ill luck in my path.
I slipped while in the bath,
Lost in a lottery,
Got cartilage in my knee.
My rich grand uncle died —
His will left me outside.
The reason why is clear,
I recollect with fear —
I knew that I had better
Send on that last chain letter!

THE TABLES TURNED

In summer our street was a bower
Of lovely trees. At any hour,
The shade was luscious, deep, and cool,
Inviting as a swimming pool.
We lolled on patio or lawn
Until the sun's last rays were gone.

But come October, how we curse —
No inundation could be worse
Than leaves that fall from those same trees
That brought relief each summer breeze.
We rake, we sweat, we heap leaves high;
We think of selling — but who would buy?

Now, treeless dwellers go on jaunts
To visit all their autumn haunts,
While we are tied at home with leaves
A host of garbage bags receives,
And rue the days we took our ease
In careless comfort beneath those trees!

POST-CHRISTMAS COMMENT

The tree is dismantled; the parties are over.
We've had indigestion, from Baby to Rover!
The students have all drifted back to their college
With more or less extra-curricular knowledge.
Christmas is over. Let's have a thanksgiving —
Three cheers for return to more normal living!

MODERN COURIER

Fleet courier with metal wings,
Like him the ancient poet sings,
You travel fast and carry far
The latest news of games and war.
In weather unsalubrious
Your handle-barred caduceus
Summons the world before my door
And furnishes my breakfast store
Of fresh-carved news on a juicy page —
Young Hermes of the atomic age!

OCTOBER THAW

We had Thanksgiving early — pumpkin pie,
And turkey with all the trimmings. This is why:
Someone left the freezer door awry.

BRIEFLY SPEAKING

Women's styles would cause no grief
If men's dislikes were not so strong —
No doubt when Eve put on the leaf,
Adam thought it was too long!

A MODERN LULLABY

Rock-a-by, baby in your new bed,
A pillow of H2O under your head.
If a pin pricks, the water will fall,
And wet will be baby, mattress, and all.

THE SELF-ASSURED

In Janet, self-assurance is at its height —
She answers all the quiz show questions; then,
So sure she is of always being right,
Works crossword puzzles with a fountain pen!

A SECOND THOUGHT FOR JULY

Invitations extended
In the glow of December
Somebody somewhere
Is sure to remember.

NEW LINES TO AN OLD STANZA

O wad some Pow'r the giftie gie us
To be unseen whan ithers see us!

RELATIVELY SPEAKING

Folks who boast of kith and kin
Wish some kin might not have been.
Folks who boast of kin and kith
Spell it Smythe instead of Smith.
Folks who boast of their relations
Never shall have my oblations,
So forget 'em if you've got 'em —
Every tub's on its own bottom!

CAUTION

Life has lovely things to sell,
But she drives her bargains well;
So be cautious when you buy —
Even Love may come too high!